Interpreting
Christian Holiness

INTERPRETING
CHRISTIAN
HOLINESS

by

W. T. PURKISER

BEACON HILL PRESS OF KANSAS CITY
Kansas City, Missouri

First Printing, 1971

*Printed in the
United States of America*

Preface

Christian holiness has three aspects. There is a grace to receive, a style of life to be lived, and a truth to be understood. It is with the truth or doctrine of holiness that we are here concerned, together with some of its implications for life.

The doctrine of Christian holiness is the conviction that, within the limitations of our humanity, the sanctifying grace of God is sufficient to free the Christian heart from the power and presence of inner sin, to fill it with pure love for God and man, and to impart power for Christian life and service in this present world. The provision for this gift of grace is found in the sacrifice of Christ on the Cross, and its dynamic is the fullness of the Holy Spirit.

The purpose of this little volume is to interpret the theory and practice of holiness in some of its biblical, historical, theological, psychological, and sociological facets. It is an attempt to do what we are charged to do in I Pet. 3: 15-16, "But sanctify the Lord God in your hearts: and be ready always to give an answer to every man that asketh you a reason of the hope that is in you with meekness and fear: having a good conscience; that, whereas they speak evil of you, as of evildoers, they may be ashamed that falsely accuse your good conversation in Christ."

Christians have a twofold task in relation to their faith. The task is, first, proclamation. It is, second, interpretation. We must proclaim the truth to those who have never heard. But we must also explain the truth to those who have heard but need to understand it more adequately.

Candor compels us to confess that we have generally been stronger on proclamation than we have on explanation. We have insisted to all who would hear that the will of God is their sanctification. We have not always been as clear as we might in telling them what it means to be sanctified.

There is a vast difference between explaining a truth and explaining it away. Some calls for "reinterpretation" seem not so much the desire for better understanding as the wish to get rid of the truth entirely. But we must be interpreters, not corruptors. We are to be translators, not transformers, of the truth. We are to explain and apply the doctrine, not change its content.

Like a city set on a hill that may be approached from different directions and by different paths, the full truth of Christian holiness must be sought in a variety of contexts.

The approaches considered here are not the only interpretations that might be given. But they represent areas in which most of the major questions arise for which we are commanded to give an answer to those who ask.

W. T. PURKISER

Contents

I. The Biblical Interpretation of Holiness   9

II. The Historical Interpretation of Holiness   19

III. The Theological Interpretation of Holiness   30

IV. The Psychological Interpretation of Holiness   45

V. The Sociological Interpretation of Holiness   59

Reference Notes   69

CHAPTER I

The BIBLICAL Interpretation of Holiness

ALL CHRISTIAN TRUTH must be based on the teaching of the Bible. God has spoken in the Scriptures and has made known to us both His will for our lives and His provision for our needs.

No important Bible truth depends on scattered and isolated proof texts. One man is said to have claimed that he could prove atheism from the Bible. He offered the text, "There is no God." What he did not say was that the context reads, "The fool hath said in his heart, There is no God" (Ps. 14:1).

The doctrine of Christian holiness is based upon the total thrust of the Scriptures. It is not merely a thread or line of truth running through the Word of God. It is rather a network of teaching which is an essential part of the fabric of the whole.

Holiness has its proof texts—although it would be more correct to call them data—evidences which support the conviction that sanctifying grace is real in human life. They should not be ignored. But even more important is the message of the whole. Behind clichés and stereotypes based on a few isolated passages is the rich and varied teaching of the Bible itself.

Before turning to the biblical presentation of holiness, it should be noted that there are two sets of English terms in the King James Version used to translate a single Hebrew word in the Old Testament and a single Greek word in the New Testament.

One of these sets of English terms comes from the Germanic roots of our language. It includes the verb "to hallow, make holy," the noun "holiness," and the adjective "holy."

The other set of English terms is derived from the Latin roots of English. It includes the verb "to sanctify," the noun "sanctification," and the adjective "sanctified."

Theologians sometimes make distinctions between these two sets of English words. For example, *sanctification* is sometimes defined as the act or process whereby a person or thing is made holy; and *holiness* is defined as the state or condition resulting from the act or process of sanctification. But since the two sets of words from which *sanctification* and *holiness* come are alternative translations of single terms in the original biblical languages, it is better to regard as equivalent expressions the verbs "to sanctify" and "to make holy," the nouns "sanctification" and "holiness," and the adjectives "sanctified" and "holy."

I

The Bible is an amazingly realistic Book. It describes with great faithfulness the sorrows and sins, the struggles and hopes, the weakness and pain of the men and women who walk its pages. Yet through it all there shines a light of redemption and victory, the light of that "holiness, without which no man shall see the Lord" (Heb. 12:14).

In swift strokes, the early chapters of Genesis paint the

picture of creation and catastrophe, holiness given and holiness lost.

Genesis 3 tells us of the source of that corruption of our moral natures for which sanctification is the divine cure. Created in the image of God, but using the freedom which was part of that image to seek to "be as gods" (Gen. 3:5) themselves, Adam and Eve brought upon their descendants the corruption that comes to a branch cut off from the source of spiritual life in the Vine (cf. John 15:1-6).

The man created in the image of God "begat a son in his own likeness, after his image" (Gen. 5:3) whose "every imagination [*yetzer*, tendency, propensity, direction] of the thoughts of his heart was only evil continually" (Gen. 6:5; 8:21). The sinful condition of the race is due to the depravity that comes from "deprivity," that is, human nature apart from the life of the Spirit.

Yet such is the marvel of God's love and patience that the very scene of human rebellion was the occasion for the first promise of divine redemption, of One who at the cost of His own suffering would crush the serpent's head (Gen. 3:15; Rom. 16:20).

Through long centuries of preparation, the fact of God's holiness was revealed in a dozen different ways—by His wonderful works, by the awe men felt in His presence, by the ritual and sacrifices of Tabernacle and Temple, as well as by the prayers, aspirations, and proclamations of those men to whom God made himself known. God was seen to be, in Isaiah's favorite phrase, "the Holy One of Israel" (1:4; 5:19; 10:20; etc.). Holiness was seen to be the very inwardness of God's being. It is His nature, His "Godness."

Equally strong was the call for men who walked with God to be like Him in moral character. In the Old Testament, the familiar biblical term "sanctify" (102 times in various forms) often has the meaning we have come to attach to "consecrate." This is clearly true when men are told, as they frequently are, to sanctify themselves; to sanctify places, garments, altars, vessels, days, priests, and people to the Lord. The meaning is to separate or set apart as dedicated to God.

This is not the whole story, however. Present from the beginning, and growing stronger through the centuries, was the recognition that people who belong to God are not only consecrated but are to be different in a real and personal way. Ritual purity is symbolic of moral purity. The repeated command, "Ye shall be holy; for I the Lord your God am holy" (Lev. 11:44-45; 19:2; 20:26), makes no distinction between the holiness of God and the holiness of His people, and is set in the context of moral conduct in I Pet. 1:15-16.

It is clear, certainly, that the holiness possible to man is not a property of his own nature. It is God's gift. But even before the finished work of Christ on the Cross, it was possible for inspired writers to describe Noah as one who "found grace in the eyes of the Lord . . . a just man and perfect in his generations" (Gen. 6:8-9); to record God's command to Abraham, "Walk before me, and be thou perfect" (Gen. 17:1); and to speak of Job as "perfect and upright" (Job 1:1, 8; 2:3).

II

The sacrifices and ceremonies that make up so much of Exodus, Leviticus, and Deuteronomy had a dual purpose. They were object lessons in the need for a blood-sprinkled way into the "holiest of all," the redemptive presence of the Lord God. And they pointed ahead to the Cross—the coming of the Lamb of God, who was to bear away the sin of the world (John 1:29).

The Psalms give us one of the best measures of the piety of the Old Testament, the type of character possible to men who walk with God. There are many insights into the nature of God's holiness and its demands upon those who worship Him (15:1-2; 24:3-4). The Psalmist distinguishes between his sins and transgressions—the iniquities he has done (51:1, 3-4, 9)—and the disposition behind the deeds, the inward "sin" for which the only remedy is the purging blood and the washing that brings a clean heart (51:2, 5-6, 10).

Old Testament teaching about the godly life came to full flower in the prophets. There was Isaiah, already a prophet (1:1 in comparison with 6:1), who experienced the taking away and purging of his "iniquity" or "sin" (note the singular), and who pointed the way to the age of the Spirit which was to come (6:1-8; 32:15, 17; 35:8-10; 44:3; 59:19, 21; 62:12—with the solemn warning of 63:7-10).

There was Jeremiah, who wrote of the "new covenant" (31:31-33; cf. Heb. 10:14-22); Ezekiel's promise of the cleansing to come from the "new spirit" within (36:25-26, 29); Joel's famous prediction of Pentecost (2:28-29); Zechariah's vision of the "fountain . . . opened for sin and for uncleanness" (12:10; 13:1, 9); and Malachi's prophecy of the Messiah's refining fire to purify and purge and make possible "an offering in righteousness" (3:1-3).

While holiness in the Old Testament did not come up to the full-orbed truth of the New Testament, the ideal is clear and the promise is sure. Its fulfillment in Christ and the age of the Spirit is the apex of the new covenant.

III

The Gospels present God's purpose for His people in two ways: in their record of the Life that must forever be the ideal for Christian aspiration, and in the teachings of Jesus and the inspired men who recorded His words.

Jesus spoke of the blessedness of the pure in heart (Matt. 5:8). He called the children of God to perfection of love (Matt. 5:43-48; 22:35-40; Mark 12:29-31; Luke 6:40).

He taught that the source of evil is the depravity of a carnal heart (Mark 7:21-23) in contrast with the emphasis on the outward or cultic holiness of the scribes and Pharisees.

Christ promised the Holy Spirit as rivers of living water to those who believed (John 7:38-39), the Father's Gift to those of His children who ask (Luke 11:13). He spoke of "another Comforter" to be given to those who love Him and keep His commandments, a Bestowment whom "the world cannot receive" (John 14:15-17).

Jesus prayed for His own (John 17:9) and for those who would believe on Him through their word (17:20) that God would "sanctify them" (17:17)—so that His joy might be fulfilled in them (17:13); that they might be kept from the evil (17:15); that they might be made perfect in one (17:21, 23); that the world might believe (17:21, 23); and that they might be with Him at last and behold His glory (17:24).

Our Lord's parting command was to tarry in the city of Jerusalem (Luke 24:49) until baptized with the Holy Spirit (Acts 1:5)—a baptism which follows the water baptism that seals repentance (Matt. 3:11-12; Luke 3:16-17; John 1:33; Acts 11:15-16) and which empowers a consistent life and witness (Acts 1:8).

The Book of Acts records the fulfillment of the promise and prayer of Jesus concerning the Holy Spirit. While the Jerusalem Pentecost of Acts 2 had an unrepeatable historical side to it as the beginning of the long-awaited "age of the Spirit," its deeper personal meaning is attested by the Samaritan Pentecost of Acts 8, the Caesarean or Gentile Pentecost of Acts 10, and the Ephesian Pentecost of Acts 19.

Few are disposed to dispute the spiritual power that comes with the baptism with the Holy Spirit. Its cleansing aspect has not seemed as apparent, despite the fact that one of the meanings of the Greek term for baptism is itself "cleansing."

The matter is settled beyond reasonable doubt, however, in Acts 15:8-9. This is Peter's testimony as to what happened to Cornelius and the people of his household: "And God, which knoweth the hearts, bare them witness, giving them the Holy Ghost, even as he did unto us; and put no difference between us and them, purifying their hearts by faith."

Although there had been speaking in other languages in Caesarea as in Jerusalem (10:46), Peter did not mention this at all. When he was concerned to show the identity of the Gentile Pentecost with what happened in Jerusalem, the only "sign" he appealed to was the fact that God purified by faith the hearts of those upon whom the Holy Spirit came.

IV

The Epistles of the New Testament, Pauline and General, give full expression to the truth of Christian holiness. It must be remembered that the letters of the New Testament are all addressed to Christians. They were written from within the context of faith, and directed to those who had been converted.

For this reason, there is no effort on the part of the writers to identify sanctification as a work of grace following conversion or the new birth. The readers are assumed already to have passed from death to life. Whatever is urged upon them must, therefore, be understood as part of what follows the initial experience of salvation. God's redemptive work in its totality is the theme of the New Testament letters. It is expressed in many ways:

a. Christians must experience in reality what is implied in baptism and provided by the Cross (Rom. 6:1—7:6).

b. Both the law and human willpower are futile in dealing with inner sin (Rom. 7:7-25).

c. Only the Spirit of life can make the believer free from the fleshly or carnal mind (Rom. 8:1-13).

d. The very mercies of God call for His people to make of themselves living sacrifices (Rom. 12:1-2).

e. Spiritual infancy and carnal living rend the body of Christ (I Cor. 3:1-4).

f. More excellent than spiritual gifts is the way of divine love (I Cor. 12:31—13:13).

g. The promises of God call us to cleansing from all filthiness of the flesh and spirit, perfecting holiness in the fear of God (II Cor. 7:1).

h. The struggle between "flesh" and "Spirit" goes on until the "flesh" is crucified with its affections and lusts (Gal. 5:17-24).

i. Those chosen to be holy and without blame before God in love must put off "the old man . . . corrupt according to the deceitful lusts," and put on "the new man, which after God is created in righteousness and true holiness" (Eph. 1:4; 4:22-24).

j. Christ loved the Church and gave himself to "sanctify and cleanse it with the washing of water by the word," that it "should be holy and without blemish" (Eph. 5:25-27).

k. There is no "perfection of glory" in this life (Phil. 3:12-14), but there is a "perfection of grace" (3:15).

l. Putting off the old man and putting on the new man must lead to life on a new and higher ethical plane (Col. 3:1-13).

m. God's will and call are to holiness, entire sanctification (I Thess. 4:3, 7-8; 5:23-24).

n. Grace teaches us to deny ungodliness and worldly lusts, and to live holy lives in this present world, looking for the coming of the God-man, who gave himself both to "redeem us from all iniquity," and to purify unto himself a people peculiarly His own, "zealous of good works" (Titus 2:11-14).

o. The strong, practical emphasis of the letter to the Hebrews is the need for converts to "go on":

- to a sanctifying union with the Captain of their salvation (2:10-11)
- into the "rest of faith" (3:12—4:11)
- to become teachers of others (5:11-14)
- unto "perfection" (6:1-3)
- to the reality of Christ's sprinkled blood (9:13-14)
- into the holiest of all (10:19-22)
- following "holiness, without which no man shall see the Lord" (12:14-17)
- with Christ without the camp where He suffered to sanctify the people of God with His own blood (13:12-14). The alternative to going on is the chilling possibility of going "back unto perdition" (10:39).

p. The double-minded man, unstable in all his ways, is directed to purify his heart (Jas. 1:8; 4:8).

q. God's obedient children are to be "holy, as he . . . is holy" in every area of their lives (I Pet. 1:14-16).

r. By the promises of God, we become partakers of His nature, and thus escape the corruption in the world through lust (II Pet. 1:4).

s. If we walk in the light of God instead of the darkness of sin, we have fellowship with Him, and the blood of Jesus Christ cleanses from all sin. To deny the need for such cleansing is to deceive ourselves (I John 1:7-8).

t. In the perfection of love, there is boldness in the day of judgment (I John 4:17-18).

Putting all this together, one can hardly escape the almost boundless optimism of the New Testament writers as they reflect the possibilities of grace. They are fully aware of the tensions involved in living godly lives in this present world in bodies that still await the full redemption of the sons of God. They know that it is through tribulation we enter the

Kingdom. Yet they thrill to the reality of the resurrection life even in the stresses, partialities, and incompleteness of the present age.

One of the crucial issues in discussions of the "higher life" portrayed in the New Testament is always the *nature and extent of deliverance* from inner sin, the old nature. "Eradication" is a term sure to be questioned. We are told that it is not a biblical term—and indeed it is not, exactly in that form—although the idea comes through rather clearly in Heb. 12:14-15.

But is it necessary to contend for a term? If anyone objects to "eradication"—and there are some overtones to the word that say more than we mean—then why not just settle for biblical language and talk about crucifixion, destruction, mortification, putting to death, putting off, purging, cleansing, purifying, or making clean? Really, it all comes out at the same place.

If we interpret Christian holiness biblically, we shall not concern ourselves with a single group of words—"holy," "holiness," "sanctify," "sanctification." We shall also stress the baptism with or fullness of the Holy Spirit; the risen or resurrected life with Christ; the righteousness of the law fulfilled in us; circumcision of the heart; salvation to the uttermost—or in Luther's sparkling phrase, "through and through"; the fullness of the blessing of the gospel of Christ; purity of heart and power for witnessing; and so on and on.

We shall turn to other interpretations of Christian holiness. But all of them must finally rest back upon the teachings of the *Holy* Bible with its clarion call "not unto uncleanness, but unto holiness" (I Thess. 4:7).

CHAPTER II

The HISTORICAL Interpretation of Holiness

CHRISTIAN HOLINESS not only has a basis in the Bible; it also has a history in human understanding. God's truth never changes. Men's understanding of that truth does change. Theology, like all other human disciplines, is constantly changing—pushing forward, and sometimes regressing.

It is because important insights are often lost that we need a basic acquaintance with the history and literature of the Wesleyan movement. Generations, like groups of people within any generation, may become provincial and cut off from the experience and thought of the Church universal.

One of the major problems of our age is its rootlessness, its lack of any sense of continuity with its past. Part of this, as Kenneth Keniston has pointed out, is due to the rapidity of change in these times in which we live. Because change comes so fast, we suffer an intensification of the present—a heightening of the "now" until we have come to talk about the "now generation," the "now people." We are, as Keniston described it, "stranded in the present."[1]

Traditionally, to be sure, church people are a conservative crowd. Most of us dislike any change we can't jingle in our pockets. But change is with us, and Thomas Wolfe was most certainly right when he wrote, "You can't go home again . . . to your childhood . . . back home to the old forms and systems of things which once seemed everlasting but which are changing all the time."[2]

But having conceded this much to the present and the changing future, we still need the perspective that comes from at least some awareness of the past. Not all the brilliant theologians and Bible scholars have been born in the twentieth century by any means. The same advice might be given to theological reconstructionists that has been offered to young protesters against the "Establishment": "Don't scuttle the ship before you have learned how to build a raft."

A sense of history provides the correctives needed for some of our one-sidedness. We need the balance that can be found in many of the older holiness classics, such as:

John Wesley, *A Plain Account of Christian Perfection*
Hannah Whitall Smith, *The Christian's Secret of a Happy Life*
A. M. Hills, *Holiness and Power*
Daniel Steele, *The Gospel of the Comforter* and *Milestone Papers*
J. A. Wood, *Perfect Love* and *Purity and Maturity*
H. A. Baldwin, *Holiness and the Human Element*
Thomas Cook, *New Testament Holiness*

And the sound, practical wisdom of George D. Watson, Samuel Logan Brengle, S. A. Keen, Beverly Carradine, and a dozen more.

Men are still writing, and in the Kingdom the new wine may be as good as the old. But the past has insights in it which we need to correct some of the overcompensations we have made—the swing of the pendulum past center point.

Two items are particularly important in the present.

I

One is the common, modern version of Wesleyan "eternal security." It differs from Calvinistic eternal security in that it relates to entire sanctification rather than to justification and the new birth. It is the notion that in the experience of holiness we have a sort of deposit of grace sufficient for the rest of life, and that sanctification is an end to be gained which when reached insures an easy slide down the slope into the Pearly Gates.

Put in such bald terms, no one would own up to such a view. But in one form or another it is surprisingly common among holiness people. Here the historical interpretation of Christian holiness can help.

Let us hear again the words of John Wesley, and let us inscribe them on the fleshy tables of our hearts:

> The holiest of men still need Christ as their prophet, as "the light of the world." For he does not give them light, but from moment to moment: the instant he withdraws, all is darkness. . . . God does not give them a stock of holiness. But unless they receive a supply every moment, nothing but unholiness would remain.[3]

If the Bible makes anything clear, it is that the cleansing which is the heart of holiness is not only a cleansing that begins at a definite point of consecration and faith, but it is also a cleansing which continues moment by moment. This is the meaning of the verb tenses in I John 1:7, which literally reads, "If we are walking in the light as He is in the light, we are having fellowship one with another, and the blood of Jesus Christ His Son is cleansing us from all sin." It begins to cleanse, and it keeps right on cleansing completely and continuously.

The experience of entire sanctification is not an end but a beginning, not a goal but a starting place. True, it is an end of carnal strife and confusion within the soul. It is an arrival at a realization of God's will for all His people.

Yet the end of carnal strife and confusion is for the sake of a beginning of peace and victory. And the point of arrival is but a portal that leads onto a highway stretching across all of life and on into eternity.

We do not retain the grace of God by hoarding it, like the man in the parable—wrapping it in a napkin to bury for safekeeping. We retain it by risking it in the marketplace, investing it in the commerce of human life, spending it freely on others in the assurance that it will return increasing dividends.

The light is present as long as the windows are open to the sun. The holiness to which God calls us is the sanctifying presence of the Lord of Glory moment by moment.

Puzzles as to "how carnality gets back into the heart" of a person who backslides after he has been sanctified are completely artificial. If the light is lost, "all is darkness." Without a supply of holiness every moment, "nothing but unholiness would remain." Carnality returns as blindness comes when sight is lost, as poverty returns when a fortune is squandered, as disease recurs when the laws of health are violated, and as death and corruption invade a branch when it is cut off from the vine (John 15:1-6).

Holiness is not a storage battery to be used whenever and wherever, apart from the ultimate source of its energy. Holiness is a throbbing, pulsating connection with the divine Dynamo.

Holiness is not a tank of water. It is a pipeline directly into the Reservoir.

This is the truth in May Whittle Moody's familiar lines:

> *Dying with Jesus, by death reckoned mine;*
> *Living with Jesus, a new life divine;*
> *Looking to Jesus till glory doth shine,*
> *Moment by moment, O Lord, I am Thine.*

Moment by moment I'm kept in His love;
Moment by moment I've life from above.
Looking to Jesus till glory doth shine,
Moment by moment, O Lord, I am Thine.

Hannah Whitall Smith in *The Christian's Secret of a Happy Life* says that, in the ongoing life of holiness, our part is continual surrender and continual trust.[4] There is a "once-for-all" surrender in the moment of full consecration, and there is a "once-for-all" act of appropriating faith. But the going and growing life in the Spirit requires that we continually surrender and continually trust.

Holiness is not only a work of grace; it is the workings of grace. It is not only an act of God; it is a relationship begun at a given time and place and renewed and maintained day by day.

This is so familiar to us in human relationships that it is hard to see why we find the idea so difficult in our relationship with God.

There is, for instance, an obvious difference between a wedding and a marriage. The wedding is a "once-for-all" event, permanently identified with a time and place, a calendar and a geography. The wedding is unrepeatable. By its very nature, it establishes what both God's law and human ideal intend to be a permanent union.

But the marriage is not a "once-for-all" event. It is an ongoing relationship.

When the wedding is over, there is nothing more we need to do about it. But we have to work at the marriage.

The wedding may take place in church or chapel. The marriage is lived daily in the home, and its implications pervade every other possible association between men and women in the shop, the office, the school, the marketplace, or wherever people are together.

Need it be said that homes which fail do not fail at the

time of the wedding, but in the course of the marriage? The test does not come during the beauty of the wedding. The test comes when "moonlight and roses turn to daylight and dishes." The test comes after the "billing and cooing," when there are too many bills and not enough "coos."

"Which things," as Paul would say, "are an allegory."

All that is true about the wedding, and more, is true about the moment when the child of God first enters the fullness of the blessing of the gospel of Christ. It is "once-for-all." It begins what is meant to be a permanent state of affairs. It has a time and a place. It is complete. It alters everything that happens, every relationship and every decision, from that time on until the end of life.

And all that is true about the marriage, and more, is true of the processes wherein God works in us to will and to do of His good pleasure. The life of holiness is a daily life in the home, the shop, the office, the school, the marketplace. It is not history; it is biography. It is never completed. It never ends.

Just as one cannot have a marriage without a wedding, so one cannot have the ongoing life without the experience of grace that initiates it. But just as the wedding has little value unless it is followed by a sound marriage, the experience of grace doesn't mean much unless it is the beginning of a deepening and ever richer relationship.

Oswald Chambers wrote, "The test of life 'hid with Christ in God' is not the experience of salvation or sanctification, but the relationship into which these experiences have led us."

Chambers went on to explain that "experience is absolutely nothing if not the gateway only to a new relationship. The experience of sanctification is not the slightest atom of use unless it has enabled me to realize that the experience means a totally new relationship. The experience may take a few moments of realized transaction, but all the rest of life goes to prove what that transaction means."

The problem, Chambers said, is that "people stagnate because they never go beyond the image of their experiences into the life of God which transcends all experiences.

"We must beware," he warned, "of turning away from God by grubbing amongst our own experiences."[5]

II

A second item wherein we may learn from history lies at the opposite end of the spectrum from the matter just considered. It is the view commonly held today that a single act of sin in the sanctified life immediately cuts off the soul completely from God and plunges it into total rebellion and complete depravity once more.

Here again the Wesleyan classics can help us. The older holiness writers—and by this I mean such people as S. A. Keen, G. D. Watson, Daniel Steele, M. L. Haney, Hannah Whitall Smith, Thomas Cook, and Beverly Carradine—almost without exception said that a sanctified Christian involved in an unpremeditated act of sin (what Thomas Cook called a "surprise sin") could be immediately forgiven and fully restored by confessing that sin and receiving forgiveness through our divine Advocate with the Father.

This view is based directly on I John 2:1-2, "My little children, these things write I unto you, that ye sin not. And if any man sin, we have an advocate with the Father, Jesus Christ the righteous: and he is the propitiation for our sins: and not for ours only, but also for the sins of the whole world."

These verses are set in the context of one of the finest expressions of cleansing from all sin and all unrighteousness in the New Testament (I John 1:6-10). Nor are they in conflict with the strong statements of I John 3:6-9, where the grammar shows that repeated sins are in mind.

The purpose of John's writing in fact is "that ye sin not" (verse 1)—and the grammar is such as to imply, "not even a single time." The apostle chooses his words carefully. He does not say, "*When* every Christian sins," or even, "*When* any man sins." The sin is not expected. There is no suggestion that it is necessary. The statement is, "*If* any man sin," and the conditional form of the statement implies the possibility of its opposite.

Yet when defeat comes, when there is an impulsive and unpremeditated transgression of God's law, the case is not hopeless. There is an instant remedy. Immediate confession brings immediate forgiveness and cleansing. Christ is the "Mercy Seat" for His own in the moment of tragic defeat as well as "for the sins of the whole world."

It is true that some have not recognized this possibility. They have suffered a bit, perhaps, from what someone has called "hardening of the categories," and have been quite vehement in the claim that a single act of sin under any circumstances plunges the sanctified soul into complete depravity and necessitates a definite two-stage restoration involving forgiveness followed later by entire sanctification.

 The result of this hardened view is one of two extremes. On the one hand, the Christian trapped into sin may go into despair and throw over his entire covenant with Christ, lapsing into total backsliding. Or, more commonly but even worse, he may cover his sin, rationalize, excuse, or deny it, and thereby drive it into his subconscious. There it festers and poisons the soul and comes out in legalism, rigidity, and a critical, judgmental, suspicious, and defensive attitude toward everybody and everything. Other people must be torn down in order to build up the crippled ego. In extreme cases, actual physical collapse takes place for which there is no medical cure. For while the conscious mind may reject the truth, the heart does not forget.

What we need to remember was said by the "fathers" in many ways:

John Wesley: "A believer may fall, and not fall away. He may fall and rise again. And if he should fall, even into sin, yet this case, dreadful as it is, is not desperate. For 'we have an Advocate with the Father, Jesus Christ the righteous.'"[6]

M. L. Haney: "One act of disobedience brings defilement, and with it comes the consciousness of impurity, and the only refuge is immediate flight to Christ, that the stain may be washed out. Satan will tempt you to throw away all that God has previously done for you, and send you back to the beginning to repent and believe for justification, and the substitution of a new consecration for the former one, that you may believe and be sanctified. . . . Don't listen to him; but *go straight to Christ with that one offence, and let him heal the wound thus made, and you will again be pure in his sight.* If you delay, you will be almost certain to add other offences, for one sin paves the way to another, and every moment of delay increases your danger. Therefore hasten while the wound is fresh, and be healed in Christ's all-cleansing blood."[7]

S. A. Keen: "There may come spiritual failures to the fully-saved soul, such as temporary disobedience, inadvertent yieldings to temptations, impulsive indulgences in wrong feelings, occasional lapses into sin. . . . The anchor that can hold the soul in this fierce storm, is to know that such spiritual repulses do not forfeit the gracious state of cleansing from all sin, unless they come from a preceding repudiation of its consecration and trust, or are immediately followed by the cancellation of the same. The soul must know, whenever such spiritual calamities come, that an immediate confession to God, and a reassertion of its trust in the all-cleansing blood, will prevent the forfeiture of its experience, and bring an immediate renewal of the witness to full salvation."[8]

Hannah Whitall Smith: "In this life and walk of faith, there may be momentary failures [defined in the context as conscious, known sin], which, although very sad and greatly to be deplored, need not, if rightly met, disturb the attitude of the soul as to entire consecration and perfect trust, nor interrupt, for more than the passing moment, its happy communion with its Lord."[9]

Daniel Steele: "So long as love to God is the undiminished motive there can be no career of sin. But faith may become weak and love may decline. Then under the pressure of temptation the child of God may commit a single sin, as [I John] 2:1 implies, and have recourse to the righteous Advocate with the Father, and thus retain his birthright in the kingdom of God. Or he may with Judas pass out of the light into so total an eclipse of faith as to enter upon a returnless course of sin entirely sundering him from the family of God, and enrolling him as a 'son of perdition,' a 'child of the devil,' whose characteristics he has permanently taken on."[10]

None of this is to excuse sin or treat it lightly. It ought never to happen in the sanctified life. But if it does, it must be dealt with honestly and forthrightly. We have been much less open and clear about this whole matter than our fathers, and much to our detriment.

It must be recognized, to be sure, that there is premeditated sin, calculated and presumptuous, which is in itself an indication of a backslidden heart. A person so involved, however, had long since lost the sanctifying fullness of the Spirit. When he comes back after his sad journey to the far country, he comes as a rebel to be forgiven and restored. He must then make his consecration anew and receive anew the fullness of the blessing of the gospel.

Even in such a case, there need be no more than a

moment of time between the renewed sense of forgiveness and prayer for the cleansing touch.

Without obscuring some real differences between piety in the Old Testament and in the New, this is what happened in David's restoration after his sin with Bathsheba as recorded in Psalms 51. Here, with but a moment between, is the prayer for forgiveness of specific sins and transgressions (verses 1-4), and the plea, "Purge me with hyssop, and I shall be clean: wash me, and I shall be whiter than snow. . . . Create in me a clean heart, O God; and renew a right spirit within me" (verses 7-10).

CHAPTER III

The THEOLOGICAL Interpretation of Holiness

THEOLOGY" IS a forbidding word to many. It suggests hairsplitting and dry-as-dust distinctions without end.

But theology is a very important part of the total Christian enterprise. It is, by definition, the systematic arrangement and exposition of truth about God and man in redemption. It seeks to bring religious truth into a coherent pattern in which each fact or datum finds expression. It is concerned with wholeness, with relatedness.

A theological interpretation of holiness will point out its lines of connection with every other major truth in Christian doctrine.

I remember a discussion years ago with Dr. H. Orton Wiley, author of the monumental, three-volume *Christian Theology*. The discussion concerned a course in the college curriculum dealing particularly with the doctrine of holiness.

Dr. Wiley objected. "How can you teach the doctrine of holiness without relating it to the doctrines of sin, salvation, the Holy Spirit, Christ, the atonement, grace, love, and all the rest?" he asked.

There was no answer.

The truth is that every major theme in Christian theology is important for an understanding of holiness. No truth stands alone. It is supported by, and has implications for, every other truth in the whole system of doctrine.

There is a new interest among theologians today in the doctrine of sanctification as it develops in the New Testament. Such is the contention of William Hordern, president of the Lutheran Theological Seminary in Saskatoon, Canada, in the chapter entitled "Sanctification Rediscovered" in Volume I of *New Directions in Theology Today*.[1] Dr. Hordern writes:

> An important development in recent theology is a renewal of interest in sanctification. The theological analysis of Christian salvation is often divided into justification and sanctification. Justification deals with how a man becomes a Christian. It describes God's forgiving acceptance of the sinner and the sinner's response of faith. Sanctification is the act of God whereby the forgiven man is made righteous, it describes how a man grows in his Christian life.

Dr. Hordern goes on to comment that this new theological concern with sanctification comes at a very appropriate time in the history of the Church. There is abroad in the world today a widespread wave of criticism directed against the life and practice of the Church, as contrasted with former criticisms of its teachings.

During the fifties of this century, as Hordern notes, the Church, in America at least, "sailed on a wave of popular approval." There was little serious criticism. "Happily, for the sake of the church's soul," Dr. Hordern writes, "those days have passed."

From within and without, organized Christianity is being subjected to searching criticism. There are deep doctrinal issues being raised. But more painfully, it is the life and practice of the Church which is being challenged most seriously.

Because sanctification is that aspect of salvation that deals primarily with the character and life of the Christian, the challenges of today are leading theologians to take a new, long, hard look at the biblical teaching about this neglected subject. Sanctification has to do with the inner changes the grace of God makes. In words that are correct as far as they go, justification is "Christ for us," while sanctification is "Christ in us."

Bonhoeffer, Brunner, Barth, and DeWolf, as well as the "new conservatives," are among those cited as having shown special interest in taking a "new look at the doctrine of sanctification."

There is in all of this a broad use of the term "sanctification." Yet the closing paragraph of Hordern's chapter is noteworthy:

> The concern for sanctification, as we have discussed it, transcends theological schools of thought. Those who are dedicated to it are not in complete agreement with one another. But the fact that men of different theologies and backgrounds are converging on this doctrine indicates that it represents an area of vital concern to theology and the church today.

It is this convergence of "men of differing theologies and backgrounds" and the surprising unity of opinion among them in defining sanctification theologically that should be underlined here.

R. H. Coats wrote in *The Encyclopedia of Religion and Ethics:* "In general, sanctification is the work of the Holy Spirit of God, in delivering men from the guilt and power of sin, in consecrating them to the service and love of God, and in imparting to them, initially and progressively, the fruits of Christ's redemption and the graces of a holy life."[2]

Presbyterian Kenneth J. Foreman wrote in *The Twentieth Century Encyclopedia of Religious Knowledge:*

> In Protestant thought, sanctification is the name given to what in Roman theology is called infused grace; but with a

difference. In the latter, grace is conceived as a force, sometimes all but impersonal; in the former, sanctification is a continuing activity of God by his personal Spirit. Sanctification is what makes goodness possible; it is not the good and gracious acts of men, but that operation of the Spirit which produces these acts.[3]

Southern Baptist Charles A. Trentham wrote: "Sanctification is thus the perfecting of the Christian life or the progressive cleansing of the soul."[4]

Dr. Charles Hodge is recognized as one of the leading Calvinistic theologians of the nineteenth century. He wrote: "Sanctification, therefore, consists in two things: first, the removing more and more the principles of evil still infecting our nature, and destroying their power; and secondly, the growth of the principle of spiritual life until it controls the thoughts, feelings, and acts, and brings the soul into the image of Christ."[5]

Admittedly, these definitions stress the progressive element in sanctification, and some of them imply that it cannot be completed during the course of this earthly life. But all agree that the goal of sanctification, as it has been understood in Protestant theology of all schools, is the removal of the principle of evil still infecting the nature of the believer, or complete deliverance from sin. All agree that sanctification is not identical with nor effected at the time of justification. And all agree that there is a sinful nature remaining in believers which must be dealt with.

It is this which brings into special significance the truth of I Thess. 5:23-24, "And the very God of peace sanctify you wholly; and I pray God your whole spirit and soul and body be preserved blameless unto the coming of our Lord Jesus Christ. Faithful is he that calleth you, who also will do it."

There are instances in the New Testament where the context shows the sanctification described to be ceremonial or partial and incomplete (cf. Matt. 23:17, 19; I Cor. 1:2; 6:11; 7:14; I Tim. 4:5; Heb. 9:13; and I Pet. 3:15).

Where such indication is lacking, we should consider the sanctification referred to as "whole" or "entire" in the Pauline sense in I Thess. 5:23. Such uses include John 10:36; 17:17, 19; Acts 20:32; 26:18; I Cor. 1:30; Rom. 6:19, 22; 15:16; Eph. 5:26; I Thess. 4:3, 7; II Thess. 2:13; I Tim. 2:15; II Tim. 2:21; Heb. 2:11; 10:10, 14, 29; 12:14; 13:12; I Pet. 1:2; and Jude 1.

Four specific themes in theology have particular bearing on our understanding of Christian holiness:

I

Central to the Christian faith are the *atoning death and the victorious resurrection of the Lord Jesus Christ.* The Cross is the focal point for all that distinguishes true Christianity from both its rivals and its imitations.

It is a strange fact, as the late Vincent Taylor pointed out, that all theological discussions of the Cross relate to justification—how the death of Christ makes possible the forgiveness of our sins.

Yet the New Testament makes it clear that the atonement has as much to do with sanctification as it does with justification. "Christ also loved the church, and gave himself for it; that he might sanctify and cleanse it with the washing of water by the word" (Eph. 5:25-26). "By the which will we are sanctified through the offering of the body of Jesus Christ once for all. For by one offering he hath perfected for ever them that are sanctified" (Heb. 10:10, 14). "Wherefore Jesus also, that he might sanctify the people with his own blood, suffered without the gate" (Heb. 13:12).

It is by the provision of a real cleansing of the heart from the stain of racial sin that the Cross becomes vital in our understanding of holiness. The writer to the Hebrews asks in one of his great rhetorical questions, "For if the blood of bulls and of goats, and the ashes of an heifer sprinkling the unclean, sanctifieth to the purifying of the flesh: how much more shall the blood of Christ, who through the eternal Spirit offered himself without spot to God, purge your conscience from dead works to serve the living God?" (9:13-14)

I John 1:6-7 also makes the same point: "If we say that we have fellowship with him, and walk in darkness, we lie, and do not the truth: but if we walk in the light, as he is in the light, we have fellowship one with another, and the blood of Jesus Christ his Son cleanseth us from all sin."

In these passages, we have a real inner cleansing as contrasted with the "positional holiness" or "holy in Christ" view made so popular by the widely used Scofield Bible. The doctrine of positional holiness is, in brief, that the believer's sanctification is not an impartation of the divine nature to him, freeing him from inner sin, but is an imputation of Christ's righteousness by virtue of which God counts him holy in spite of the continued corruption of his heart.

One brother is alleged to have testified in prayer meeting: "The righteousness of Christ in my life is like a beautiful, white covering of new-fallen snow in a barnyard hiding the filth and corruption of my heart."

Someone in the back spoke up: "Yes, Brother, but what do you do when the thaw comes?"

This is a proper question because the thaw always comes.

In its actual development, the "holy in Christ" theory leans heavily on the fourth chapter of Romans, in which it is stated that "Abraham believed God, and it was counted unto him for righteousness" (verse 3). It is assumed that "for" means "instead of," and that Abraham's faith was a substitute for a righteous character.

But God does not deal in fictions. When God counts a

man righteous, it is because His grace has *made* him righteous. "For" as used here means "as a condition of" or "as a requisite for."

There is a basic misunderstanding of the very words Paul used. "To count, reckon, or impute" are all English translations of a Greek word which, as C. Ryder Smith has pointed out, is a bookkeeping term and means "to take account of what is."[6] Paul's point here is that Abraham's righteousness was an asset he had received without earning it by works. But it was an asset that was genuine and real, not fictional or imaginary.

When a bookkeeper enters figures on the asset side of the balance sheet, those figures represent values which actually exist. To put down sums as assets for which there are no corresponding realities is one of the ways embezzling is done. Men go to jail for such practices as this.

God is most certainly not the cosmic embezzler. His books are accurate and true. What He imputes, He imparts. He does not whitewash—He washes white through the blood of His own Son.

The basic issue is whether the righteousness and holiness of which the Bible speaks is fiction or fact, imputed—but not actually given—or imparted. Peter's statement at this point is clear and forceful: "As he which hath called you is holy, so be ye holy in all manner of conversation; because it is written, Be ye holy; for I am holy" (I Pet. 1:15-16). There is nothing fictional or imaginary about the holiness of God. Nor is there anything fictional or imaginary about the divine nature He imparts (II Pet. 1:4).

Even more specific is John's statement about those who have hope of seeing and being like the Lord at His appearing: "And every man that hath this hope in him purifieth himself, even as he is pure" (I John 3:3). The purity of the believer is to be the same in quality as the purity of the Saviour.

There is no suggestion that a human being will become like God in His infinity and deity. A single ray of sunshine is never the sun itself. But each ray shares the light and purity of the sun. The likeness is a matter of quality, not quantity. But it is a real likeness.

It is through the atonement that the prayer of the Psalmist is answered in the provision of the Saviour: "Purge me with hyssop [the desert shrub with which the blood of the sacrifice was sprinkled], and I shall be clean: wash me, and I shall be whiter than snow" (Ps. 51:7), is answered with the assurance, "The blood of Jesus Christ his Son cleanseth us from all sin" (I John 1:7).

II

Another theme at the heart of theology is *the doctrine of the Holy Spirit.* Overshadowed in historical theology by the doctrines of the Father and the Son, the doctrine of the Spirit has come to new recognition within the past few decades.

The theology of the Holy Spirit is crucial for an understanding of sanctification. Christian holiness is *bought* by the blood of the Cross. It is *wrought* by the Holy Spirit applying the merit of that Blood to the cleansing of the heart.

Everything in Christian experience from the earliest dawn of conscience down to the resurrection from the grave comes to us through the agency of the Third Person of the Trinity. Daniel Steele rightly called Him "the Executive of the Godhead."

a. The Holy Spirit is the Source of conviction for sin and the earliest interest in things spiritual (John 16:7-11).

b. The Holy Spirit brings into human life the power for righteousness which is regeneration, "the new birth" (John 3:3-7).

c. The Holy Spirit gives us His witness to sins forgiven and sonship to God (Rom. 8:15-17).

d. We are led through the Christian life by the Spirit (Rom. 8:14), and He guides us into all truth (John 16:13) and helps us pray as we ought (Rom. 8:26-27).

At the Last Supper, Jesus made five historic statements concerning the Holy Spirit—passages that have come to be known as "The Paraclete Sayings" from the Greek term *Parakletos,* translated "Comforter" (John 14:15-18, 26-27; 15:26-27; 16:7-11 and 12-15).

The first "saying" summarizes the whole. That there is a dispensational or historical aspect to these words is, to be sure, true. But the whole tone of the Last Supper discourse, as well as the specific extension of the prayer of John 17 to "them also which shall believe on me through their word," makes its truth the heritage of believers in every age and clime.

It is Christ's own who are addressed. Those who love Him will keep His commandments (John 14:15). For such, He will pray the Father, "and he shall give . . . another Comforter" (verse 16). A *parakletos* is literally "one called alongside to help"—a helper, an advocate, a counsellor, one to support, hearten, and strengthen. "Another" implies that Jesus himself had already been such to them.

The *Parakletos* is "the Spirit of truth." People identified with the world cannot receive Him, although He convicts them; and when they repent and believe, He regenerates them and begins to dwell with them (verse 17). "With" and "in" do not mean "outside" and "inside" as a first glance might indicate—for verse 23 uses "with" in the same sense as "inside." Rather to "dwell in" means to take up a fixed and settled abode—to "abide with you for ever" (verse 16).

This "abiding forever" is identified in Acts 1:5 as being "baptized with the Holy Ghost" and in Acts 2:4 as being "filled with the Holy Ghost." It is a far cry from the transient and fleeting presence implied in the idea of "breathing out" in daily confession of sins and "breathing in" the Holy Spirit.

It is the Spirit's fullness that fully sanctifies. Sanctification is identified in the New Testament as being the special work of the Holy Spirit (Rom. 15:16; I Thess. 4:7-8; II Thess. 2:13; and I Pet. 1:2).

The continuity of the Holy Spirit's work in Christian experience must always be kept in mind. The new birth is a "birth of the Spirit." He is the young Christian's Guide and Witness (Rom. 8:14-17). "You know him," Jesus said to His disciples before Pentecost; "for he dwelleth with you" (John 14:15-17).

Holiness is the result of the "baptism with" the Spirit, the fullness of the Spirit. One hesitates to put too much weight on the language of metaphor. But there is an obvious difference between birth and baptism. And in the order of grace as well as the order of nature, birth must of necessity precede baptism.

Nor is there any puzzle as to how the same Spirit may be at one time the Source of regeneration and later become the Source of entire sanctification. He is the same Person in a different relationship. A man may have the same girl as first his fiancée and later his bride. A man may have the same doctor first as his physician and later as his surgeon. It isn't a matter of more or less of the girl or more or less of the doctor. It is a matter of the relationship and of the function.

III

The doctrine of sin is central in Christian thought. A theologian's stance in regard to the nature of sin tends to color and control his whole thought about God, man, and salvation. To minimize sin is to minimize the Saviour. To misunderstand sin is to misunderstand salvation. Sin is the source of our whole human predicament.

One of the clearest distinctions in biblical theology is the distinction between sins as acts or deeds, and sin as an attitude or disposition. Our human problem in regard to sin is twofold. It is the problem of the wrongs we have done, the guilt we have incurred—what Paul had in mind when he wrote, "All have sinned, and come short of the glory of God" (Rom. 3:23). But it is also the problem of what we are, the nature we have inherited—estranged from God, corrupted, and bent toward evil. This is what Paul meant when he spoke of the "sin that dwelleth in me" (Rom. 7:17).

The new birth, experienced in any genuine conversion to Christ, puts an end to sinning when understood as avoidable transgressions of the revealed will of God. Some have broadened the idea of sinning to include mistakes, unavoidable faults and failures, lapses of memory, or unconscious deviations from perfect righteousness. But to do this makes nonsense of such scriptures as John 5:14; Rom. 6:1, 15; I John 2:1-4; 3:6-10; and 5:18. If God means what He says, then regenerating grace stops a career of sinning.

But the new birth does not end the problem of inner sin—sin as attitude, disposition, propensity, or tendency. The New Testament witnesses to this in many ways. There is an echo in the justified life of the struggle Paul describes in Rom. 7:14-25, a struggle not entirely ended until the position described in Rom. 8:2-4 is reached.

The carnal mind is enmity against God (Rom. 8:7). Even babes in Christ experience its presence (I Cor. 3:1-3). Unsanctified Christians need to cleanse themselves of all filthiness of flesh and spirit, perfecting holiness in the fear of God (II Cor. 7:1). "Flesh" and "Spirit" are locked in unrelenting struggle until the "flesh" is "crucified . . . with the affections and lusts" (Gal. 5:17, 24).

The "old man" as the corrupt cause of the former manner of life must be "put off" (Eph. 4:20-24; cf. Rom. 6:6).

Sinful dispositions and tendencies are to be put to death (Col. 3:5-7).

God's people must beware of an evil heart of unbelief, the potential cause of backsliding and apostasy (Heb. 3:12). The root of bitterness springing up troubles the believer. Following peace with all men, and holiness, is the cure (Heb. 12:14-15).

There is a double-mindedness resulting in instability and cured only in the purifying of the heart (Jas. 1:8; 4:8).

"Sin in Believers" as John Wesley used the phrase[7] consists not in the choices they make or acts in violation of God's law they commit. It exists as a latent condition or state, a principle or propensity rather than an activity. It is variously described as the carnal mind, the mind of the flesh, the flesh, the old man, the root of bitterness, the seed of sin, indwelling or inbred sin, original sin, or depravity.

It is with this problem of inner sin that entire sanctification deals. The result is what Scripture describes as a "pure heart" (Matt. 5:8; Acts 15:8-9; Titus 2:13-14; Jas. 4:8; I Pet. 1:22; I John 1:7; 3:3). The baptism with the Spirit thoroughly purges (Matt. 3:11-12). Our "old man" is crucified so that the "body of sin" might be destroyed (Rom. 6:6-7). The "Spirit of life in Christ Jesus" makes us free from "the law of sin and death" (Rom. 8:2-4).

To "be holy" may mean much more but it can never mean less than to "be cleansed" or "made free from" the taint of sinfulness. Only on these terms can we serve God "in holiness and righteousness all the days of our life" (Luke 1:73-75), "holy and without blame before him in love" (Eph. 1:3-6), "blameless and harmless . . . without rebuke" (Phil. 2:14-16), enjoying a religion that is "pure" and "undefiled" (Jas. 1:27), "holy in all manner of conversation [living]" (I Pet. 1:14-16), "without spot, and blameless" (II Pet. 3:14).

Unless we are to think of God as making impossible and therefore unreasonable demands upon His children, we must recognize that "all His commandments are enablings."

In fact, those who deny the reality of cleansing from sin face a rather impossible dilemma. If God purposes to purify the hearts of His people and *cannot,* He is not the infinite God the Bible reports Him to be. On the other hand, if God can purify the hearts of His people and will not, He is less than holy, taking more pleasure in sin than in righteousness. Neither alternative can be accepted.

The whole tenor of the scriptural revelation of God supports the view that He is both able and willing to fulfill His promises—breathtaking though they may be. If it be not "thought a thing incredible . . . that God should raise the dead" (Acts 26:8), it should not be thought incredible that His people would be enabled to walk "in newness of life" (Rom. 6:4).

IV

The great word of both the Bible and theology is salvation. While we have drifted into the habit of identifying "salvation" or "being saved" with conversion, the true meaning of the term is far greater. The New Testament uses the term "salvation" to describe the whole consequence of Christ's redemptive work in human lives.

Salvation in the Bible, therefore, has a past, a present, and a future. We *have been* saved by grace through faith (Eph. 2:8; II Tim. 1:9). We *are being* saved by the power of the Cross (I Cor. 1:18; II Cor. 2:15, cf. Greek). We *shall be* saved when Christ comes again (Matt. 10:22; Acts 15:11; Rom. 13:11; Heb. 9:28; I Pet. 1:3-5). Salvation is free (justification); it is full (entire sanctification); and it is final (glorification).

In a special way, the human name of our Lord conveys

the idea of salvation: "Thou shalt call his name JESUS: for he shall save his people from their sins" (Matt. 1:21). The term *from* is quite emphatic here, and it is a word that suggests deliverance from without. In no possible way can it be considered as meaning "in," "with," or "among."

It is with the idea of salvation from the presence and power of inner sin that we are concerned here. W. E. Vine gives as one of the meanings of "salvation" in the New Testament "the present experience of God's power to deliver from the bondage of sin. This present experience on the part of believers," he says, "is virtually equivalent to sanctification."[8]

In a similar vein, Ryder Smith claims that "it goes without saying that Paul's exposition of such terms as 'justify' and 'sanctify' is an exposition of salvation."[9]

That salvation in its full and unqualified sense includes sanctification is seen rather clearly in II Thess. 2:13, "But we are bound to give thanks always to God for you, brethren beloved of the Lord, because God hath from the beginning chosen you to salvation through sanctification of the Spirit and belief of the truth." Salvation is "*through* sanctification of the Spirit," not "as a preparation for" sanctification.

Titus 2:11-14 also shows that the salvation which comes from the grace of God includes both redemption from all iniquity and the purification unto Christ of a people for His own, marked by their zeal for good works. This is not something to be achieved in a future life, but to enable us to "live soberly, righteously, and godly, *in this present world.*"

Heb. 7:25 says, "Wherefore he is able also to save them to the uttermost that come unto God by him, seeing he ever liveth to make intercession for them." The Phillips translation most accurately catches the meaning of the phrase "to the uttermost" as being "fully and completely."

It is of salvation in this full sense that it has been said:

God thought it.
Christ brought it.
The Spirit wrought it.
The Blood bought it.
The Bible taught it.
The devil fought it.
Love sought it.
Faith caught it.

And happy the Christian who can say,

I've got it!

CHAPTER IV

The PSYCHOLOGICAL Interpretation of Holiness

For BETTER OR FOR WORSE, we live in an age that is incurably psychological. The post-Freudian world can never be the same as the world before Freud. This is not all bad. Whatever we can learn that will help us understand the nature of man will help us understand a little better the experience of holiness.

Just as archaeology and secular history have shed light upon places and events reported in the Bible, so the sciences of human nature—psychology, anthropology, sociology— may help us understand better what it was God created when He formed man of the dust of the earth and breathed into him the breath of life, so that man became a living soul fashioned in the image of his Maker.

Theology itself has felt the impact of psychology. Archbishop William Temple, who anticipated so much that has come to the fore in contemporary theology, wrote: "Our theology has been cast in a scholastic mould, i.e. all based on logic. We are in need of and we are gradually forced into, a theology based on psychology. The transition, I fear, will not be without much pain; but nothing can prevent it."[1]

It is only necessary to add that if the psychology upon which such theology is based is biblical psychology the gain will be great.

I

Never should we underestimate the divine element in our sanctification. What God does in and for us is nothing short of a miracle. Yet right along with this is another truth that needs to be brought into focus. Divine grace does not cancel our humanity.

We still live in an imperfect world, conditioned by a hundred factors over which we have no control, some of which go back into infancy and early childhood. And God works within the limits of that humanity.

"We have this treasure in earthen vessels," wrote the Apostle Paul (II Cor. 4:7). I have never had the temerity of the seminarian who took this as his text and spoke in his preaching class on "The Glory of the Cracked Pot." But the truth is, some of the vessels are chipped, some of them are marred, and some of them *are* a bit cracked.

Psychology can help us understand better the complexity of our motivations, the degree to which our reactions are conditioned by past experiences, the way in which apperception actually alters our grasp of truth, and the unsuspected ways in which the unconscious colors and affects conscious experience. It may aid us in freeing ourselves from the myth that people always react alike and are equal in temperament and personality.

Our psychological age should also alert us to the need to be careful in our modes of expression. Carelessness in the use of psychological terms sometimes involves us in saying what we do not mean.

A prime example of this is the term "self." We sometimes talk about the eradication or destruction of "self." We know what we mean, or at least it is to be hoped that we do. We mean self in the sense of "selfishness." We mean the eradication or destruction of the sinfulness of the self. In this sense we may talk about "self" being "crucified and slain, and buried deep, and all in vain may efforts be to rise again." In this sense we understand the prayer we sometimes hear, "Lord, slay the self in me."

But self more properly means the real inner being, the ego, the central core and soul of personal identity. It is the "I," the "me," that persists through all modifications and changes from birth to death. If this psychological ego were to be crucified or destroyed in any literal sense, the result would be nonentity.

Whatever else it is, carnality is the human self corrupted, diseased, fevered, and warped. Holiness cleanses the corruption, heals the disease, takes away the fever, and straightens the warp. But it does not destroy the self. That self must be consecrated and cleansed and committed to the purposes of God.

Paul the Apostle expressed it all in one of his great paradoxes: "I am crucified with Christ: nevertheless I live; yet not I, but Christ liveth in me: and the life which I now live in the flesh I live by the faith of the Son of God, who loved me, and gave himself for me" (Gal. 2:20). Here, as Dr. William Greathouse has so well expressed it, is a sinful "self" to be crucified with Christ, a human self to be controlled by Christ, in order that the true self may be realized in Christ.

E. Stanley Jones testified: "I laid at His feet a self of which I was ashamed, couldn't control, and couldn't live with; and to my glad astonishment He took that self, remade it, consecrated it to Kingdom purposes, and gave it back to me, a self I can now live with gladly and joyously and comfortably."[2]

Such a surrender is the heart and soul of Christian consecration. Consecration is not chiefly the surrender of possessions, things, or even other people. It is the submission of the central self to the sanctifying will of God. Possessions, things, and others are involved in the believer's consecration. But it is only when the final "Yes" is said which permanently admits the Saviour to the innermost recesses of the soul that consecration becomes real and complete.

This is the insight expressed in the order in Frances Ridley Havegal's familiar "consecration" hymn. Life, hands, feet, voice, lips, silver and gold, will, heart, and love are all presented in that sequence. The process might go that far and still fall short were it not for the final, climactic gift of all:

> *Take myself and I will be*
> *Ever, only, all for Thee.*

The radical, uncompromising claim of Christian consecration is sketched in clear outline by the late C. S. Lewis in his spiritual autobiography, *Surprised by Joy.* When he turned from atheism to Christianity, he found, so he said, that "there was no region even in the innermost depth of one's soul (nay, there least of all) which one could surround with a barbed-wire fence and guard with a notice, No Admittance. And that was what I wanted; some area, however small, of which I could say to all other beings, 'This is my business and mine only.'"[3] But God would not be satisfied with less than all.

The self is not to be slain. It is to be surrendered. It is the "vessel unto honour" of which Paul wrote: "sanctified, and meet for the master's use, and prepared unto every good work" (II Tim. 2:21). What makes the difference is that self is no longer on the throne, pretending to be the lord of the life. Self is in the servant role, on its knees, consecrated to the Lord of all life—no longer central but submissive.

II

The distinction between humanity and carnality is of prime importance for a psychological interpretation of holiness. Theoretically, it is not hard to state the difference. Practically, one man's "humanity" may be another man's "carnality," and what would be condemned as carnality in others may be excused as humanity in oneself.

Objections to the possibility of holiness usually fall into one of two classes. Either it is claimed that human nature as such is sinful or it is said that the source of sin is in the physical body.

Neither of these views is defensible. Those who claim that human nature as such is sinful have a twofold problem on their hands. They must either hold that God did not create Adam and Eve as truly human or else that He created them as sinful beings. And they must either hold that the sinfulness of human beings is eternal or that the redeemed will be transformed into something other than human when they enter heaven.

Neither pair of alternatives is very promising. Adam and Eve were created in the image of God in innocence and primitive holiness, untested but still real. They were created as human beings. The very name "Adam" means "man."

Nor do the finally redeemed become anything other than human beings in heaven. The Saviour, who took upon Him the nature of man, is still "the man Christ Jesus" (I Tim. 2:5), although exalted to the right hand of God. In the new heavens and the new earth, the dwelling of God shall be with men and they shall be His people (Rev. 21:3).

The view that the seat of sin is the physical body is equally mistaken. It is true enough that many of the sins common to human life are those which come through the pull of bodily appetites and desires. Yet in the 17 works of the flesh listed by Paul in Gal. 5:19-21, the majority have no physical basis whatsoever—as, for example, "idolatry, witchcraft, hatred, variance, emulations, wrath, strife, seditions, heresies, envyings."

The idea that the body is sinful also runs head on into the doctrine of the incarnation. Every evidence in Scripture points to the fact that Jesus of Nazareth, the sinless, holy Son of God, had a normal human body. He grew hungry and tired; He slept; He ate; He rejoiced; He suffered; He was subject to every kind of temptation we have, "yet without sin" (Heb. 4:15).

Sin in human nature is an intrusion. It does not belong in man as he was designed to be. It is no necessary part of anything essential to a full and normal human life.

But where is the dividing line between the human and the sinful? How can one tell the difference between those tendencies, inclinations, and desires which are part of our necessary human existence and those which come from and together constitute the nature of inbred sin?

There is an important clue in the statement about "the mind of the flesh" in Rom. 8:6-7, "For to be carnally minded is death; but to be spiritually minded is life and peace. Because the carnal mind is enmity against God, for it is not subject to the law of God, neither indeed can be."

In the phrase "not subject to the law of God, neither indeed can be" we have the line of distinction drawn. Whatever is human within us—part of man's normal psychological makeup—can be and is subject to the law of God. Whatever is carnal is not and cannot be subject to God's law.

In fact, the entire purpose of the moral law is to give guidance and direction to human nature and its varied expressions. Every human instinct, need, and desire has a possible legitimate expression within the guidelines laid down by God's law. Each of the Ten Commandments, for example, establishes limits and guidelines for human tendencies which are legitimate and right in their proper place.

On the contrary, no carnal impulse, attitude, or tendency can find an expression in Christian life within the law of God. None is subject to His law. All are outlaw propensities and inevitably lead to sin.

Consider the sorry list: envy, malice, animosity, bitterness, retaliation, selfish temper, pride, covetousness, grudge holding, lovelessness, divided loyalty, double-mindedness. How can one be envious or malicious in keeping with the law and nature of Christ? How can one manifest animosity and bitterness in harmony with Christian ideals? Even to ask the question is to see the answer.

Human psychological impulses and tendencies, as Paul said of the physical body, are to be "kept under" (I Cor. 9:27). All carnal impulses and tendencies, on the other hand, are to be eliminated by that divine conditioning of our selfhood by the indwelling Spirit, who alone enables us to love God supremely and our neighbors as ourselves.

III

Involved in the psychological interpretation of holiness is the need to learn to live with limitations. We all have to walk the narrow path between the too easy acceptance of our limitations and the futility of constantly beating our heads against a stone wall. Some too quickly surrender to their obstacles. They accept as inevitable what they should attack and overcome. Others make themselves and everyone around them miserable by a hopeless struggle against limitations in their lives they should learn to accept.

It is important that we rightly measure our limitations. Some of them we may overcome by direct action and with the help of God. Others we must come to terms with and learn to live with.

There are limitations in the measure of health and strength. There are limitations in education and training. There are limitations in native ability and talent. There are limitations that come with advancing age. And there are limitations in circumstances, past and present. A man cannot lift himself by his bootstraps when he has no boots.

The New Testament has a comprehensive word for limitations. It is the word "infirmity," and it literally means lack of strength, weakness, or "inability to produce results."

Paul, more than any other New Testament writer, speaks of infirmities. He gives us the promise that the Holy Spirit "helpeth our infirmities" (Rom. 8:26). While the particular weakness in view is lack of knowledge about what to pray for, the term is plural and the statement is general.

The very word "help" is full of meaning. When a person promises to help us with something, it does not mean that he is going to do it for us. The only way we can need help is to be doing something too big to be done alone.

Sometimes limitations can be taken away. More often, we climb on top of them.

Paul, again, is our teacher. Whatever his "thorn in the flesh" may have been, it seems almost certain it was a physical fact. The apostle prayed three times for deliverance—and the idea is clear that these prayers were not casual wishes beamed Godward, but prolonged and intense seasons of supplication.

When the answer came, it was not exactly as the apostle had expected. But it satisfied him fully. Christ said to him, "My grace is sufficient for thee: for my strength is made perfect in [your] weakness."

Then Paul gives us our best secret for successfully living with limitations. He said, "Most gladly therefore will I rather glory in my infirmities, that the power of Christ may rest upon me" (II Cor. 12:8-9).

This is turning liabilities into assets. When one is not so gifted, he works harder. When one cannot run like a hare, he plods like a tortoise—and usually comes in ahead.

We can, to be sure, put up with our limitations. We can accept them and suffer them. But it is better to use them for stepping-stones and climb over them. We grow by working away at the edges of our liabilities. We may not completely overcome them. But if we face them honestly and bravely, we shall find that in the long run we are both bigger and better for the effort.

IV

The best of saints still have a long road to travel. There are rough places to be smoothed, kinks of mind and personality to be straightened out, failings and weaknesses to be faced, corrected, and strengthened.

As James McGraw has well put it, "Psychological weakness is not necessarily spiritual wickedness." One may have the baptism with the Holy Spirit and still need help with personal problems of emotional adjustment.

We must not forget that people may be pure in heart but immature in personal development. Paul described the aim of the Christian gospel as not only "the perfecting of the saints" but also "that we may henceforth be no more children, tossed to and fro, and carried about with every wind of doctrine" and that we may "grow up" (Eph. 4:12-15).

Sanctified people may have problems with prejudices that have been drilled into them from early childhood until they have become a stubborn part of their entire outlook on life. One has only to recall Peter's struggle over establishing fellowship with Gentile Christians, as reflected in Acts 10 and Gal. 2:11-14, to see a vivid illustration of this. When Peter was sanctified at Pentecost, he didn't lose his Jewish prejudices overnight.

Sanctified people may have problems that arise from differences of judgment, or from the emotional conditionings of close family ties. We have but to remember the disagreement between Paul and Barnabas over John Mark (Acts 15:36-41) to see this.

Without the Spirit's help, we could never cope with our human weaknesses effectively. Without the indwelling Spirit, Peter never would have conquered his prejudices, nor would he have written about "our beloved brother Paul" (II Pet. 3:15) after Paul took him to task for them. Without the openness of perfect love, Paul never would have conceded that John Mark had vindicated himself (II Tim. 4:11).

But the problems still arose and had to be faced. If they had not been solved, they could have defeated the purpose of God in the lives of Peter, Cornelius, Barnabas, Mark, and Paul. Without the Holy Spirit, they *could* not. Without their honest effort, He *would* not.

V

Important to the psychology of the sanctified life is an understanding of the place and function of emotions in our humanity. Many seem to expect an experience of constant joy and blessing. Because peace with God and the witness of the Spirit to a clean heart often find expression in high emotional tides, some have tended to make feelings an indicator of the spiritual state.

The problem is, of course, that emotions have a way of changing from day to day. They are affected by factors that have no relationship whatsoever to one's spiritual and moral condition. There is nothing but danger in identifying feelings with the grace of God.

Even Jesus is described as "a man of sorrows, and acquainted with grief" (Isa. 53:3), whose tears flowed when He was confronted with the sorrow of His friends and the hardness of those He had come to help (John 11:35; Luke 19:41). Paul confessed his continual heaviness and sorrow of heart for his own nation (Rom. 9:1-2), and found occasion to need encouragement from Christian friends (Acts 28:15).

Peter writes to those "who are kept by the power of God through faith unto salvation ready to be revealed in the last time. Wherein ye greatly rejoice, though now for a season, if need be, ye are in heaviness through manifold temptations: that the trial of your faith, being much more precious than of gold that perisheth, though it be tried with fire, might be found unto praise and honour and glory at the appearing of Jesus Christ" (I Pet. 1:5-7).

John Wesley wrote:

> A will steadily and uniformly devoted to God is essential to a state of sanctification; but not a uniformity of joy, or peace, or happy communion with God. These may rise and fall in various degrees; nay, and may be affected either by the body or by diabolical agency, in a manner which all our wisdom can neither understand nor prevent.[4]

Emotion and blessing play an important part in Christian life. A religious experience which had no effect on the feelings would not meet the needs of the whole person. It would not go far enough.

But the purpose of emotion in religion is akin to the purpose of emotion in other areas of life. It is not primarily to be enjoyed. It is to be employed. It is the natural prelude to action.

There is more in common between "emotion" and "motion" than the fact that the two words differ by only one letter. God has given us physical feelings, for instance, as part of the preparation for some sort of physical action. Fear is a good example. In fright, the glands pump additional adrenalin into the bloodstream, the heartbeat is quickened, and the body is prepared for "fight or flight."

Conversely, the appropriate action strengthens the emotion which corresponds to it. Running away increases the fright. Clenching the fists strengthens anger. Whistling tends to lift the spirits.

The application of this to the spiritual life is not difficult to see. God gives high tides of blessing and joy, not simply for the sake of making us happy, but to prepare us for service to the Kingdom and to our fellowmen. Just as emotion in the physical life can actually be harmful unless followed by action appropriate to it, so blessing and spiritual joy miss their purpose unless they work out in heightened devotion. Emotion which is not expressed in devotion eventually dries up.

But the very best state of grace will not guarantee high emotions all the time. Holiness is not hilarity. Feelings are a by-product of spirituality and neither its cause nor its measure.

C. W. Ruth used to say, "Feelings are the most undependable dependence anyone ever depended on!" He would comment that the only man in the Bible who went by "feeling" was Isaac, who as a result blessed the wrong boy!

Faith is the supreme condition for salvation. Holiness is a relationship based, not on feeling, but on faith. Faith anchors to facts: the fact of God's promises, and the fact of consecration and obedience. Feelings are swayed by circumstances, and may have no direct relationship to the facts whatsoever.

Feelings are conditioned by the physical tonus of the individual. The state of health and the condition of one's nerves make a great deal of difference in the emotions he has.

Two excerpts from the journal of a pioneer New England circuit rider serve to illustrate this point. The first entry is dated Wednesday night at bedtime:

> Arrived at the home of Brother Brown late this evening, hungry and tired after a long day in the saddle. Had a bountiful supper of cold pork and beans, warm bread, bacon and eggs, coffee and rich pastry. I go to rest feeling that my witness is clear; the future is bright; I feel called to a great and glorious work in this place. Brother Brown's family are godly people.

But the next entry, written late on Thursday morning, tells a different story:

> Awakened late this morning after a troubled night. I am very much depressed in soul; the way looks dark; far from feeling called to work among this people, I am beginning to doubt the safety of my own soul. I am afraid the desires of Brother Brown and his family are set too much on carnal things.[5]

Because feelings vary, will and purpose must govern our lives and not feelings and impulse. Every Christian must learn to do what is right whether he "feels like it" or not.

Conviction, not convenience, must be our guide to conduct. It is well to go to church, to serve in the Kingdom, to read the Bible, and to pray—when we "feel like it." It is better to do these things whether we feel like it or not.

While we cannot always account for the fluctuation of our moods and the changing tide of emotions, we need not surrender to them. The peril of uncontrolled moods is discouragement, one of Satan's most powerful tools.

There are some important lessons at this point in the story of Elijah, "a man subject to like passions as we are" (Jas. 5:17). After the tremendous victory on Mount Carmel, under the threats of Jezebel, Elijah fled to the wilderness, fell under a juniper tree, and wished to die. His emotional collapse was complete. Utter discouragement filled his soul.

In this extremity, God did three things for Elijah.

First, the Lord provided for the prophet's physical needs. An angel fed him, and he slept soundly. His nerves had been stretched to the breaking point. His reserves were exhausted. Good emotional health is closely connected with good physical health.

Second, God gave Elijah normal companionship. He directed him to find Elisha and call the younger man to be his associate. The tendency of those who are discouraged is to withdraw from friends and Christian associations. This is the worst possible thing to do. One way to throw off undesirable moods is to seek the company of good Christian friends.

The third step in Elijah's recovery was the challenge of a new task. Instead of sitting and brooding over his difficulties, the prophet was given a new assignment. To be active, to find a job and do it wholeheartedly, is a sure cure for the "blues."

There are two elements more fundamental than feelings in holiness. These are obedience and faith—the two "feet" whereon the child of God must walk.

When high feelings subside, and "heaviness through manifold temptations" comes, then one should check his consecration and obedience, "dig in," and hold on by faith. Like all trials, "this, too, will pass"; and faith, so much more precious than gold, though it be tried in the fire, will "be found unto praise and honour and glory at the appearing of Jesus Christ."

CHAPTER V

The SOCIOLOGICAL Interpretation of Holiness

W<small>HAT</small> PSYCHOLOGY IS to the individual, sociology is to people in groups. There is not only a psychological approach to holiness; there is also a sociological approach to its deeper understanding.

The psychological approach to holiness considers the individual in all the richness and diversity of his personal life. The sociological approach considers the interrelations of persons in community and church. The term "sociology" is, of course, used here in a broad and nontechnical sense.

John Wesley's famous sermon on Matt. 5:13-16 has often been quoted. There is, said Mr. Wesley, no such thing as a solitary Christian. Christian life is life in community, in the fellowship of the Spirit we call the church.

There is unsuspected meaning for the people of God in the very term "sociology." It is derived from *sociare,* "to associate with," and *socius,* "a companion or associate." It is the study of the forms and functions of human association. Our literature is replete with biblical theologies and biblical psychologies. A standard work in biblical sociology has yet to be written.

The sociology of religion must consider the degree to

which our opinions and practices are conditioned by the broader society in which we live, the problem of social change, the relation of social consensus and individual conscience, the need for sorting essentials and incidentals in the marks of the Christian community. These and many others are important themes in understanding Christian holiness.

I

Holiness itself implies an awareness of and sensitivity to the social implications of the Gospel.

There was great concern for the poor and disadvantaged among early holiness people. They knew nothing of the separation between personal piety and social concern that has marked the evangelical church of the last half-century. Indeed, most of the great social reforms of the last half of the nineteenth century grew out of the work of dedicated evangelicals, many of whom were leaders in the holiness movement.

Sherwood Wirt records:

> The evangelical preacher, the revivalist, the mass evangelist, carried the doctrines of holiness and Christian perfection into the seamy aspects of the day. They revealed a boundless passion for the welfare of humanity. Anything that stood in the way of making America great—and Christian— they opposed. Thus they spoke frequently for the friendless, the jobless, the drunkard, the illiterate, the Indian and the Negro, the widow and the orphan.[1]

A century before, John Wesley had been untiring in his efforts on behalf of the poor, actually impoverishing himself in the process. His encouragement to William Wilberforce in the struggle to outlaw human slavery is well-known.

Dr. P. F. Bresee did not leave the Methodist church and ministry in a direct confrontation over second-blessing holiness—although his dedication to holiness certainly contributed to the adverse and apparently unexpected action of the bishop and the conference. It was rather through a desire to engage in city rescue mission work and to preach the gospel of full salvation to the poor.

The early holiness movement proliferated orphanages, homes for unwed mothers, hospitals, and dispensaries as well as schools and colleges.

There have been some marked changes at this point among us in the last half-century. The holiness people who in the days of the founders had been ardent proponents of the total gospel found themselves drawn more and more into the orbit of Calvinistic fundamentalism with its pietistic and negative reaction against the growing "social gospel" emphasis of early twentieth-century modernism.

Fundamentalism increasingly hardened its stance and became separatist, reactionary, and in general committed to the sort of prophetic dispensationalism that involved the church in a back-to-the-wall defensive reaction against the evils of the day. In the meantime, the liberal or modernistic wing of the American church (and within the churches) espoused the ecumenical cause and began to interpret mission and evangelism as service rather than salvation.

The result has been to leave those evangelicals who could not follow the narrow fundamentalist line with what Carl F. H. Henry has rightly called an "uneasy conscience."[2] We have the feeling that we ought not to be silent in the face of glaring social evils. Yet to speak has seemed to align us with the liberal ecumenical movement in a sort of "Me, too" echo. Even the timid and tentative gestures recently made have brought fierce cries of compromise from the ecclesiastical right wing.

What we need to recover is the insight that "personal gospel" and "social gospel" are both perversions of the New Testament. There is only one Gospel. To split it is to destroy it.

We cannot choose between doctrine and ethics, between

creed and life, between inner experience and outer conduct, between individual salvation and social action. Both are in the New Testament and are not divided. "What God has joined together, let not man put asunder."

E. Stanley Jones said it well:

> The clash between the individual gospel and the social gospel leaves me cold. An individual gospel without a social gospel is a soul without a body, and a social gospel without an individual gospel is a body without a soul. One is a ghost and the other a corpse. Put the two together, and you have a living person. I want and need one gospel—a gospel that lays its hand on the individual and says, 'Repent, be converted,' that lays its hand on the corporate will and says, 'Repent, be converted'—one gospel, two applications.[3]

II

Another topic in the sociology of holiness has to do with relationships between persons within the same spiritual fellowship. Paul gives a prime example in Romans 14. "The kingdom of God," he says, "is not meat and drink [or eating and drinking], but righteousness, joy, and peace in the Holy Ghost" (verse 17).

But this great holiness text is embedded in a discussion of one of the perennial and ever perplexing problems of the Christian community. It deals with that wide range of matters about which there is no clear word of God, and in which the consciences of equally devout people differ. The examples Paul uses are eating meat and observing the feast and fast days of the Jewish calendar.

Some are bound by scruples which they must observe. To violate their own conscientious convictions would involve them in sin.

Others do not share those scruples. These persons must be conscious of their influence.

Somewhat surprisingly, Paul identifies the scrupulous

as "weak" and those with ability to distinguish between incidentals and essentials as the "strong."

I well remember a very conscientious Christian in my home church who would not wear a necktie—that "little bundle of pride tucked up under a man's chin." So opposed to ties was he that they said he would not even sing "Blest Be the Tie That Binds"! To his credit, he never tried to get the tie off me, nor did he allow my wearing of a tie to bother him the least bit. But we never did agree on the propriety of sanctified men wearing neckties.

Paul makes the point clear. In such instances as this— and they are legion in our day as always—the weak must not judge the strong, and the strong must not hold the weak in contempt.

Blessed twice over are those who are fixed and unyielding in their adherence to essentials—the principles of the godly life—while maintaining flexibility and adaptibility in regard to nonessentials and methods. Ends must be fixed. Means must be flexible. There is a difference between being rugged and ragged. Bad manners are not necessary for true holiness. Some have never learned the difference between rudeness and reality, between boorishness and biblical standards.

Many today, both inside and outside the holiness movement, have hang-ups about holiness. But nine times out of 10, those hang-ups are the result of identifying human traditions and convictions about incidentals with the pure truth of God. Traditions are a wonderful heritage, and never to be treated lightly. But when they result in blindness to biblical principles, we must go with God.

III

A perennial problem in group relationships is the confusion of legalism with lawfulness. Legalism is the stunted and spoiled fruit of a lovely tree—a contradiction of everything true Christianity means. It limits the growth of individuals, thwarts the development of a true and unfettered conscience, and introduces bickering and bitterness into relationships within the church.

Nowhere is the true character of legalism more clearly seen than in the picture of the Pharisee the Gospels draw for us. Here is the very worst in religious personality—the smug complacency of the supposedly superior, combined with the hypocrisy used to cover the inevitable inconsistencies in such a life.

When Jesus told His famous parable of the Pharisee and the publican, He addressed it to some "which trusted in themselves that they were righteous, and despised others" (Luke 18:9). Here are clearly portrayed the two sides to the Pharisaic attitude: self-righteous pride, and judgment of others.

It is no accident that pride and judging are mentioned together. They cannot really be separated. The person who would justify himself, by the same token, must despise others. He must rise above those around, not by intrinsic worth, but by pushing others down.

Oswald Chambers, who has left the holiness movement some of its most incisive insights, gave a penetrating analysis of legalism:

> The nature of Pharisaism is that it must stand on tiptoe and be superior. The man who does not want to face the foundation of things becomes tremendously stern and keen on principles and on moral reforms. A man who is hyper-conscientious is nearly always one who has done something irregular or who is morbid; either he is on the verge of lunacy, or he is covering up something by tremendous moral earnestness along certain lines of reform.
>
> A Pharisee shuts you up, not by loud shouting, but by the unanswerable logic he presents; he is bound to principles, not to a relationship. There is a great amount of Pharisaism abroad

today, and it is based on "devotedness" to principles. . . . A disciple of Jesus Christ is devoted to a Person, not to principles.[4]

One point must not be forgotten. Pharisaism did not start as it finished. Pharisaism originated as a "hold the line" movement against the inroads of foreign culture into Jewish religious life.

The lesson is that reaction can go too far. Regardless of the area or issue, the pendulum may swing so far off center that it actually provokes the swing to the other extreme. The extreme of Pharisaism tends to drive others either into the ranks of the publicans or of the Sadducees, just as Pharisaism itself was a reaction against compromise.

Because legalism builds its case on rigid applications of certain selected parts of the law, some would do away with the idea of law entirely. But the point is that lawfulness is not legalism.

The Apostle Paul makes this unmistakably clear in the last part of the seventh and the first part of the eighth chapters of Romans. The closing verses of Romans 7 picture the inevitable failure of legalism as a basis of the spiritual life. The law fails, not because there is anything wrong with its ideals, but "in that it was weak through the flesh" (Rom. 8:3). Essentially, a legalist is a carnal man trying to live a holy life.

The "righteousness" legalism produces is itself contrary to the very law it professes to extol. For legalism wins its only semblance of success by a combination of spiritual pride and inconsistency. The inconsistencies may be ignored or denied, but they are unavoidably there.

But Paul points out that "what the law could not do, in that it was weak through the flesh," God has done by the Spirit of life in Christ Jesus—"sending his own Son in the likeness of sinful flesh, and for sin," condemning or "dooming" sin in the flesh. And all this is "that the righteousness of the law may fulfilled in us, who walk not after the flesh, but after the Spirit" (Rom. 8:4).

That is to say that the very purpose of the gospel of grace is to bring our lives into conformity with the law of God—not by external demand, but by internal dynamic. The power of the Spirit of life fulfills the righteousness of the law in us in the only way it can really be done—from within.

The law of the Lord, for the child of God, is not the rigid compulsion of an unwanted limitation. It is the road map and guide to be followed with love and joy. The true Christian fulfills the law, not as the basis of his salvation, but as the fruit of it. The lawfulness of his life is his love offering to his Lord.

Harold J. Brokke recalls a story which illustrates this truth. A woman was married to an austere, demanding, and loveless man who made her life a constant misery. Each morning he gave her a list of duties for the day and checked each evening to see that they were performed. He even wrote and posted a list of 10 rules for the house which she must obey. What love she had for him was soon crushed.

Then the man died, and the widow was released from the demands of her husband. Eventually she met and married a fine Christian gentleman. The second husband was a man of consideration and kindness, everything the first man had not been. Love reigned in the home.

One day, cleaning a bureau drawer, the lady came upon the list of rules drawn up by her first husband. Curiously, she read it. To her amazement she found that she was keeping every requirement, not out of duty but out of love!

However defective the illustration may be, the point is well made. Love is its own "law." But it is law with a difference. As John wrote, "For this is the love of God, that we keep his commandments: and his commandments are not grievous" (I John 5:3). In such a life there is lawfulness without legalism.

IV

The final proof of Christian doctrine is not its reasonableness or its logical cogency. The final proof of Christian doctrine is its embodiment in flesh and blood. If men are to see and know, the "Word" still must become flesh and dwell among them. Truth must become real in human form to be convincing.

There are, after all, two kinds of definition. There is definition by connotation—defining in terms of meanings, logical principles, genus, and species. Then there is definition by denotation—defining by pointing to an example of what one is talking about.

Peter put the two together in the passage quoted in the Preface: "But sanctify the Lord God in your hearts: and be ready always to give an answer to every man that asketh you a reason of the hope that is in you with meekness and fear: having a good conscience; that, whereas they speak evil of you, as of evildoers, they may be ashamed that falsely accuse your good conversation [or manner of life] in Christ" (I Pet. 3:14-16).

We need to give answers and reasons to those who ask. But more, we should be able to say, "Follow me, as I follow Christ."

B. T. Roberts said it strikingly years ago: "No arguments of geologists can raise the price of real estate in any section of the country so rapidly as can a well, sending up its hundreds of barrels of oil a day. Scripture proofs of the doctrine of holiness cannot convince the people that it is attainable, so unanswerably as a holy life."

It does little good to sing "I'm Dwelling in Beulah Land" and talk about milk and honey if all we have to show for it are crab apples and sour grapes. A person can be as "straight as a gun barrel" theologically and "clean as a hound's tooth" ethically and still be unpleasant and un-Christlike in spirit. Some who talk about perfect love are mean, narrow, censorious, humorless, and bitter in their personal attitudes.

But the natural fruit of the Spirit of Christ is a winsome constellation of graces with love at the core: love, joy, peace, patience, kindness, goodness, faithfulness, humility, and self-control. Only lives so governed can demonstrate the reality of holiness.

Missionaries in India say that the Hindu rejoinder to Christianity in India has gone through three stages. The first was, "It isn't true." The second was, "It isn't new." The third and most devastating rebuttal was, "It isn't you." You don't live it. You don't measure up.

What the world and the Church need now is a great cloud of witnesses to Christian holiness about whom they can say—whether grudgingly or gladly—"Your doctrine isn't new, but there must be something in it, because we've seen it in you."

Reference Notes

Chapter II

1. Quoted in Sheldon Garber, ed., *Adolescence for Adults* (Chicago: Blue Cross Association, 1969), pp. 74-75.

2. *You Can't Go Home Again* (New York: Harper and Brothers, 1941, p. 706.

3. *A Plain Account of Christian Perfection* (Kansas City: Beacon Hill Press of Kansas City, 1966, reprint), p. 82.

4. (Westwood, N.J.: Fleming H. Revell Company, reprint), p. 32.

5. *If Thou Wilt Be Perfect* (London: Simpkin Marshal, Ltd., 1949, reprint), p. 85.

6. Sermon on Matthew 5:13-16. *Works,* V, 301.

7. *The Inheritance Restored,* Fourth Edition Revised and Enlarged. (Chicago: The Christian Witness Co., 1904), p. 171.

8. *Salvation Papers* (Cincinnati: M. W. Knapp, 1896), pp. 97-103.

9. *Op. cit.,* p. 163.

10. *Half-Hours with St. John's Epistles* (Boston: Christian Witness Co., 1901), Comment on I John 3:9, *loc. cit.*

Chapter III

1. (Philadelphia: The Westminster Press, 1966). The quotations that follow in the text have been taken from the chapter indicated.

2. Edited by James Hastings (New York: Charles Scribner's Sons, 1924), XI, 181.

3. L. A. Loetscher, editor in chief (Grand Rapids, Mich.: Baker Book House, 1955), p. 1053.

4. *Encyclopedia of Southern Baptists* (Nashville: Broadman Press, 1958), p. 1184.

5. *Systematic Theology* (New York: Charles Scribner and Co., 1872), p. 221.

6. *The Bible Doctrine of Sin* (London: The Epworth Press, 1953), p. 140.

7. The title of one of Wesley's "standard sermons." Sermon XIII, *Works,* V, 144-56.

8. *Expository Dictionary of New Testament Words* (London: Oliphants, Ltd., 1940), III, 316.

9. *The Bible Doctrine of Grace* (London: The Epworth Press, 1956), p. 74.

Chapter IV

1. Quoted by J. G. McKenzie, *Psychology, Psychotherapy, and Evangelicalism.* (London: George Allen and Unwin, Ltd., 1940), p. vii.

2. *Mastery: The Art of Mastering Life* (New York: Abingdon Press, 1955), p. 97.

3. (New York: Harcourt, Brace and Company, 1955). The last two chapters illustrate this point.

4. *Letters,* VI. 68; quoted by J. Baines Atkinson in *The Beauty of Holiness* (London: The Epworth Press, 1953), pp. 131-32.

5. Leslie R. Marston, *From Chaos to Character* (Winona Lake, Ind: Light and Life Press, 1944), pp. 76-77.

Chapter V

1. *The Social Conscience of the Evangelical* (New York: Harper and Row, 1968), p. 39.

2. *The Uneasy Conscience of Modern Fundamentalism* (Grand Rapids: Wm. B. Eerdmans Publishing Co., 1947).

3. *A Song of Ascents: A Spiritual Autobiography* (Nashville: Abingdon Press, 1968), p. 151.

4. *Baffled to Fight Better: Talks on the Book of Job* (London: Marshall, Morgan and Scott, 1916 and 1955). p. 72.